THE SHOP PILOT SEASON, EPISODE 3, LOS ANGELES, CA

KITH
ye must
be Born

purple
Supreme
BIG3

THE SHOP

Where Culture Shapes Up

INSIGHT
EDITIONS
San Rafael • Los Angeles • London

Welcome to *The Shop*.

This place?

It's where the constant sound
of clippers and cuts meets real talk.

I've always said, the realest talks happen where you least expect them, like in a barber's chair, surrounded by familiar faces and a casual, laid-back vibe. That's *The Shop*.

The Shop isn't just about people talking to each other. It's deeper. It's about the things that shape us, the battles we fight, and the journey we're all on. Diving deep into what drives us, fuels our passion and the hurdles we face trying to leave our mark. It's an invitation to be a fly on the wall for the best barbershop conversations you've ever heard.

Over the years, we've peeled back the curtain, showing the world that athletes, artists, and entertainers are more than sound bites. This platform is probably the most candid you'll hear me. Before everyone had a podcast, the barbershop was where they'd open up about life, on and off the court. The talks can get a little wild in there for sure, but keeping those unfiltered, raw conversations going was always the goal. Everyone should feel comfortable, from athletes to leaders in culture, music, comedy, and beyond. Every episode resonates with people just being themselves.
The Shop has grown—seven seasons in, we've made history and become part of the culture.

See, in the barbershop, it's all about community. Growing up in Akron, single mom, only child, you know my story by now. But the barbershop was my peace, my learning ground. Before I was anybody, I soaked up stories about the game's legends, got schooled on life, the latest beats, flicks, who was the funniest, and, of course, sports talk—everything we're still talking about today.

We can't bring everyone to those Akron shops, or Cleveland, Chicago, Detroit, LA . . . but with *The Shop*, we're bringing that culture, energy, community spirit to you.

Flipping through these pages, we hope you'll feel like you're right there with us, catching every word, every emotion, every piece of advice over the past seven seasons. From sports greats to the most influential names in entertainment and culture, each voice adds to our collective story and shared journey. It's a highlight reel of our stories, showing the power of opening up and the connections made through honest conversation.

So, as you dive into these pages, embrace the realness, see your journey in ours, and find inspiration to stay true to your story, just like we do in every episode of *The Shop*.

LEBRON JAMES

SEASON 2, EPISODE 1, CHARLOTTE, NC

CONTENTS

OUR CULTURE SHAPES

FROM MUSIC TO

WE'RE NOT

WE'RE

THE WORLD.

SPORTS,

JUST

PARTICIPANTS;

TRENDSETTERS.

Maverick Carter

SEASON 4, EPISODE 1, LOS ANGELES, CA

In the tapestry of African American history, few threads are as colorful, enduring, and textured as the Black barbershop. It's a narrative that stretches beyond the simple act of cutting hair. An institution that has stood the test of time, the Black barbershop has been much more than a place to get a fresh cut; it has been a cornerstone of the community, a hub of cultural and political discourse, and a bastion of Black entrepreneurship. Black barbershops exist as a place of resistance, affirmation, and brotherhood in a world often antagonistic to the very notion of Black freedom and dignity.

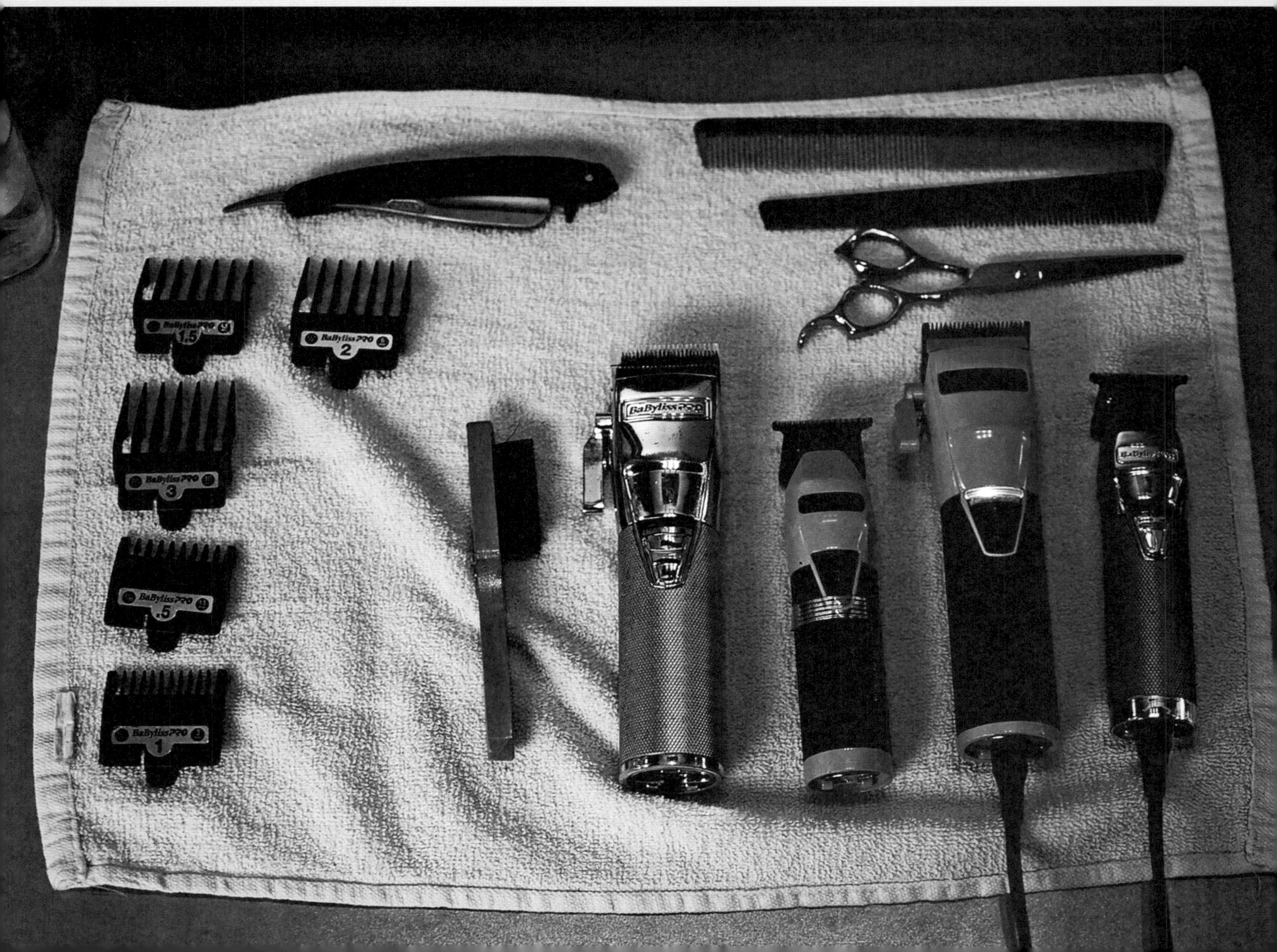

The genesis of this story is as complex as the history it carries. In the antebellum era, the art of barbering was one of the few skills a Black man could claim as his own, even though it was in servitude to white masters.

For free Black men in the North, owning a barbershop was a rare crack in the wall of economic opportunities. This business venture was left open because white folks considered barbering beneath them. Yet, paradoxically, these early Black entrepreneurs catered almost exclusively to white customers. The tides began to turn post–Civil War with the influx of European immigrants who, unconcerned by America's racial social practices, entered the barbering scene in droves. This shift, coupled with burgeoning licensing laws and the sinister spread of Jim Crow, rewrote the Black barbering narrative, prompting Black barbers to redirect their focus toward serving their communities.

By the late 19th and early 20th centuries, Black barbers began opening shops focused on Black customers. These spaces quickly became more than just places to get a haircut; they became hubs of socialization, political discourse, and communal support. In the face of Jim Crow laws and societal segregation, Black barbershops offered a haven, a private space in the public sphere. Historian Quincy T. Mills describes the Black barbershop as a place "where Black men can come to reconnect, to be themselves, and enjoy each other's company." This unique environment has fostered a sense of belonging and identity crucial in building strong, confident Black men. *The Shop* has been where status and stigmas dissolve for generations, leaving room for unfiltered conversation and camaraderie.

As the civil rights era dawned, the role of the Black barbershop shifted from a passive communal space to an active center of organization and resistance, serving as an incubator of Black political thought. As Melissa Harris-Perry eloquently illustrates in *Barbershops, Bibles, and BET: Everyday Talk and Black Political Thought*, these are the arenas where ideologies are dissected and debated. It's here that complex tapestries of political ideologies are woven.

In recent decades, the health and well-being of African American men have become a new focus within these spaces.

Recognizing that Black men often face disproportionate health risks and have a distrust of conventional healthcare systems, public health officials and researchers have turned to barbershops as culturally safe sites for health education and screenings. Successful collaborative initiatives between barbershops and healthcare agencies now address diseases such as prostate cancer, hypertension, COVID-19, diabetes, HIV, and other STDs, proving that the barbershop can serve as an effective conduit for improving community health.

The Black barbershop is a microcosm of the African American experience—a testament to resilience, a sanctuary of freedom, and a crucible for forming a collective identity. These spaces narrate a story of a people striving for dignity in a world that has often denied them the same.

As we continue to navigate a complex and often divided world, the Black barbershop remains a testament to the strength and spirit of the African American community. So, when one steps into a Black barbershop, it's more than a step into a place of business; it's a step into the heart of our life and history, a sacred space that has, time and again, proven itself to be more than just a place for a haircut.

RAWFORD GRILL

SEASON 4, EPISODE 1, LOS ANGELES, CA

THE BARBERS

The Shop is a show that maintains a direct link to the culture that created it by involving barbers, often giving real haircuts to guests or hosts as the show tapes, offering a distinctive and authentic experience for both the participants and the viewers. For the barbers who appear on the show, however, it's just another day at *The Shop*.

Vince "The Barber" Garcia, a barber for over fifteen years who has been on the show since the first episode, says,

"When a client sits in my chair, my top priority is to make them feel comfortable. We're not just there to cut hair. We're like therapists," he laughs.

Barbers like Garcia, Lionel "Brownie Blendz" Harris, and Nick "Slick" Castellanos directly link the show and the shops that inspired it. They grew up going to neighborhood barbershops and witnessed firsthand the impact a barbershop can have on its community.

SEASON 6, EPISODE 2, SALT LAKE CITY, UT

"There's something about the chair, the smell of the product that makes people automatically feel super comfortable," says Harris.

For these barbers, *The Shop* is not just a place to cut hair; it's a space for meaningful connections. "I may meet a kid when he's born. I might give him his first haircut, but then also might give him his college graduation haircut and his wedding haircut. The bond is real. There are clients who may have had three or four wives and only had one barber their whole life. They were committed to them," says Brownie.

"Our job is to build confidence. Nobody should ever feel guilty about feeling good about themselves."

Through their work on the show, these barbers showcase their skills and embody the role of therapists, providing a listening ear and a friendly presence for everyone who walks through the door. "Our job is to build confidence. Nobody should ever feel guilty about feeling good about themselves. Our job is to help people as part of our communities. Everybody needs a little help, man. Nobody can do it by himself," says Castellanos.

Nick's talent has taken him from southwest Miami to memorable moments, like during the 2016 Finals, highlighting his pivotal role in the athletes' lives: "[During the 2016 Finals] I'm sitting at the game and realize all of a sudden, I cut the hair of every single person that was playing for Cleveland and Golden State on the floor. All ten of them on the

“If there is something that you want, plan it out and execute. Don’t let anyone tell you you can’t.”

floor at the same time, and not during a blowout either,” Castellanos recalls, laughing.

Their impact weaves through their work, capturing the essence of creativity and community connection, and embodying the show’s core values of authenticity and cultural exchange. They showcase the direct line from neighborhood shops to the pinnacle of sports and entertainment.

When asked for advice for up-and-coming barbers, they all had unique answers. Brownie says to do the work. “Success comes from consistent hard work. Be the last one to leave, even during slow times. Keep working, keep honing your craft, and stay faithful.”

Castellanos challenges rookie barbers not to overlook the community aspect of the craft. “We build community. If you’re successful and put the work in, you can open up a barbershop or you can open up a barber school. It’s an opportunity to give opportunity.”

Garcia’s advice is straightforward. “If there is something that you want, plan it out and execute. Don’t let anyone tell you you can’t.”

WE WANT TO ASK QUESTIONS THAT SPARK

SEASON 5, EPISODE 2, CLEVELAND, OH

INTEREST AND HOPEFULLY SOME DISCOURSE, RIGHT?

THAT'S *THE SHOP.*

Randy Mims

"The Shop isn't just about the conversations that happen within its four walls; it's about the ripple effect those discussions have on the world outside."

Few shows have stitched together the worlds of sports, culture, and candid conversation quite like *The Shop*. The premise is simple yet revolutionary: strip away the formalities of traditional interview settings and replace them with the raw, unfiltered ambiance of a barbershop. It's in this setting where athletes, musicians, and cultural icons let their guards down, revealing truths and sharing insights that resonate.

Since its inception, the series has not only redefined the genre of sports talk but also elevated it, turning casual banter into a conduit for deeper societal discussions. Crafting such a platform was no small feat.

In this oral history, co-creators Randy Mims and Paul Rivera, joined by executive producer, Maverick Carter, pull back the curtain on the creation of the show. From the spark of inspiration to the meticulous crafting of its pilot episode, they delve into the challenges and triumphs of bringing their vision to life. It's a journey marked by unyielding commitment to authenticity, the pursuit of impactful dialogue, and the creation of a space where the veneer of celebrity fades, revealing the individual behind the persona.

The Shop isn't just about the conversations that happen within its four walls; it's about the ripple effect those discussions have on the world outside. As we dive into this oral history, Rivera, Mims, and Carter share not just the mechanics of making a show but the heart and soul that make the series a haven for unscripted truth in a scripted world.

The following peels back layers of their journey, offering insights into the ethos of the show. It's a testament to the power of conversation and the enduring relevance of the barbershop as a cultural cornerstone. Welcome to *The Shop*—where every cut, every shave, and every word has the power to shape, to define, and to inspire.

SEASON 5, EPISODE 2, CLEVELAND, OH

SEASON 5, EPISODE 8, LOS ANGELES, CA

AN ORAL HISTORY

THE SHOP: ORIGINS AND INSIGHTS

In the world of television and media, the alchemy of teamwork can transform a simple idea into a cultural touchstone.

This was exactly the case with *The Shop*, where the combined efforts of co-creators, Paul Rivera and Randy Mims, turned a concept into a cornerstone of contemporary dialogue. Both of these men brought a unique set of skills and perspectives to the table, but it was their shared vision and collective effort that breathed life into the show. Rivera and Mims were soon joined by executive producers, LeBron James and Maverick Carter, who aided the co-creators in shaping the vision for the show you see today.

Known for his sharp insights and strategic thinking, Paul Rivera's vision for *The Shop* was not just about giving athletes and celebs a voice but providing a space that mirrored the candid and often spirited discussions typical of a barbershop setting. This familiar and intimate setting strips away the usual formalities of media interviews, allowing guests to speak freely on issues close to their hearts.

SEASON 5, EPISODE 2, CLEVELAND, OH

Randy Mims, a childhood friend of LeBron James and an integral member of the athlete's inner circle, provided the project another layer of authenticity and trust. His involvement ensured that the conversations remained genuine and that the guests felt comfortable sharing their truths, no matter how vulnerable. Mims's role was crucial in maintaining the ethos of the barbershop—the spirit of community, camaraderie, and unguarded dialogue.

Joining Rivera and Mims is Maverick Carter. Often seen as LeBron James's right-hand man, Carter has long been a linchpin in sports marketing and content creation. Carter brought a unique flair to the show, transitioning from his background in marketing to becoming an on-air talent. This shift was not just a new role for him but marked a significant moment in his career, as it allowed him to facilitate conversations that went beyond sports, touching on politics, culture, and personal growth in a whole new dimension.

The history of *The Shop* begins with its first episode. This groundbreaking moment not only introduced the world to a more "unfiltered" LeBron, but also showcased the seamless dynamic between Carter and Rivera as on-air talent. Each episode since has built on that foundation, turning *The Shop* into a space where athletes and celebrities alike can share their highest triumphs and deepest anxieties.

This chapter aims to delve into the origins and impact of *The Shop* through the words of those who were there from the start—Rivera, Mims, and Carter. Their insights not only illuminate the mechanics of the show but also highlight how their personal journeys and professional experiences have interwoven to create a platform that challenges, celebrates, and changes the narrative around the lives of modern athletes.

“For me, the barbershop really became that place where I got game.”

PERSONAL BARBERSHOP EXPERIENCES

“I’m from New York City. The Lower East Side of Manhattan, to be specific. I think anyone that comes from inner cities would tell you that barbershops play perhaps the most significant role in the culture of their upbringing, right? It’s like there’s no world where you didn’t have some sort of relationship or interaction with a barbershop.

“The barbershop might be the only place in the world where, if you just panned a seating area, you’d see an executive. You’d have a high school quarterback, you’d have a mom and a kid, and you’d have a drug dealer all sitting kind of right there. I don’t think there’s anywhere else really where Americans can say that happens consistently on a weekly basis.

“My father was incarcerated when I was twelve years old. For me, the barbershop really became that place where I got game. I just learned so much being in those rooms. How to be a man, dos and don’ts, how to carry myself. How to get yourself out of trouble, things that would get you into trouble, and how to manage relationships. I think the most important thing for me that I got from a barbershop at an early age was just getting game from kind of those OGs. They’d say things like, ‘Young blood, you’re thinking about it wrong, look out for this thing. I’ve been down this route. I just came home from being away in prison. You don’t want to do that thing, that’s a dead end.’ So, for me, being that my dad was away for a large portion of my childhood, the barbershop really played a significant role in really raising me. I don’t think that’s an overstatement.”

BRINGING THE VISION TO LIFE

“We were at this restaurant in New York, downtown. I looked around. It was myself, LeBron, Steve Stoute, Maverick, a couple other people, and we were just having a dinner and Nas was there. Me, just as a massive Nas fan and a fan of music in general, it was surreal being in the room. Someone asked him, ‘Hey when you said this bar, we thought you were talking about this person.’ He’s like, ‘No what you didn’t know is that I did this thing.’ We were like, ‘My God, we’ve been listening to the music 15 years and had no clue. That’s what you were saying!’ So, that was the spirit of the conversation that night.

“The subject matter went from sports stuff to music to politics to responsibility with our platforms we have, and I had a moment in that room where I thought to myself, ‘I am genuinely learning more in this room and in these types of conversations than I learned in all my formal education.’ Actually, it would have been a beautiful thing if the 16-year-old PR had access to these types of conversations and knowledge. So that started the wheels

> "*The Shop* was created because I saw a white space of opportunity, related to the world the barbershop plays in our communities."

turning. How could I turn these conversations and protect the sanctity of them, protect the organic nature of them, where that viewer could just be a fly on the wall for this kind of conversation? That started the wheel spinning and at first, my vision for *The Shop* was gonna be a podcast.

"We were going to have those types of conversations; I was gonna invite guests from my network of relationships and have the same conversations you see now on the show. I took this idea to my business partner and co-creator, Randy, and he made my idea better.

"It was gonna be called *The Shop*, but we were gonna do barbershop talk and he was like, 'Okay, why don't we do it in an actual barbershop, and we have multiple conversations, and really create the energy [of the barbershop]?'

"It was fairly easy to get the show created because we were trying to create something bigger than a show. We were just trying to create a platform for a conversation, a platform for information, very specific to our communities that we come from.

"A good idea is simply that, a good idea. The team and the things you need to really fall into place are very challenging to do the simplest thing. I would say it was easy to get this show made, and the reason why I say it was easy to get this show made is because it was never created as 'a show.' I think a lot of times, that's the business: 'Hey, we create content; we create shows.' THAT's really hard and difficult to do. *The Shop* was created because I saw a white space of opportunity, related to the world the barbershop plays in our communities."

WHAT MAKES *THE SHOP* DIFFERENT?

"We don't ever want this thing to come off as a Q and A. We wanted it to be a rich conversation, but for that to happen at the highest level of celebrity. We've been fortunate enough to have everyone feel ownership, and everyone has to feel comfortable to engage in that conversation at every level.

"If you asked me on day one and if you asked me or Mav today, we don't consider ourselves journalists. I do think we pride ourselves on being relationship people and protecting those relationships. I'd say 95 percent of the people we have on the show, there's a relationship. Whether it's with myself, Mav, we've worked with them in some capacity, or there's just an affinity, or we're fans of the people that we have on.

"Mav and I are very clear on what our roles are; we are conductors of the conversation. We're really humming, and when we know we have a great show is when the guest themselves, they're asking questions of each other. They're asking questions, they're asking, 'Hey, can I double down on that for a second?' That's the beauty of this thing.

"If you've been to any barbershop, you don't agree with everything, and I think that's kind of the beauty of it that we've created: a safe place where people can have different opinions and discourse in a safe place. And I know our roles, we're just asking hopefully interesting questions that create dialogues and then kind of getting out of the way. And then if there are nuggets there where someone may say something, we're like, 'Hey, double down on that a little bit,' and that leads to even richer conversation.

SEASON 5, EPISODE 3, LOS ANGELES, CA

> "If you've been to any barbershop, you don't agree with everything, and I think that's kind of the beauty of it that we've created: a safe place where people can have different opinions and discourse in a safe place."

"I think when we really hit the nail on the head right, it is having an episode where you have one of the most established successes, a true Hall of Fame artist like Jay-Z in a room with an artist that shifts on the cusp of becoming that, like Bad Bunny. And if you go back and look at that episode, there's a beautiful moment that happens there when I believe it's LeBron and Jay or maybe Mav [says], 'What's it feel like when you walk off the stage? Can you go home and just be normal?' And Jay says, 'No, you can't, because you have the energy. You've just been having a two-way energy exchange with 18,000 people.' And then he looks at Bad Bunny and goes, 'In your case. It's 80,000 people. You do stadiums.' And Bad Bunny was so locked in listening to everything Jay said. If he had a notepad, he would have been writing everything down, right? He was in such awe.

"The biggest compliment I can be paid on *The Shop* is exactly that it feels like it's not an interview; it feels like you're looking at a conversation you maybe shouldn't even be privy to. And I believe that, at the core of it, we've been able to accomplish that, because we've never, since the inception, treated it like a show. We always treated it like a conversation that was important to our community. We want to ask questions that spark interest and hopefully some discourse, right? That's *The Shop*."

THE SHOP'S LEGACY

"My hope for *The Shop* is that people view it as more than just a show. That people view *The Shop* as a platform and have real dialogue and get real information. Hopefully, this will provide people with tools, whether that's insight, information, access, or opportunities.

"Ultimately, when you boil it all down, whether that's in the form of content, live experiences, or products such as men's grooming or this book, I hope what people ultimately see in *The Shop* is a mirror, right? And I think that's something beautiful about when we walk into a barbershop, the first thing you look at is yourself in the mirror and the last thing you look at is yourself in the mirror, right? I want people to look at *The Shop* and see a reflection of themselves in their community and not only that we're representing them in a manner of what they are, but, more importantly, what they want to be. And as long as we're doing that, as long as people can look at *The Shop* at every touchpoint, whether that's just watching content and laughing or being inspired, whether that's attending one of our live experiences or tours, whether that's buying and supporting one of our products and using it, I hope people feel a sense of home and a sense of community and a sense of the connection, that same feeling you get in that mirror in the barbershop."

"I wanted a place where it was comfortable for everybody, because everybody's comfortable in a barber's chair."

PERSONAL BARBERSHOP EXPERIENCES

"The barbershop in the community that we're from was part of growing up. It was like a thing where my dad took me as a kid, and we spent a day in the barbershop, and you would buy products and you would buy different foods and you learn life lessons.

"There were men in the barbershop that I looked up to, whether they were street guys, whether they were actual barbers, or they were other people's parents. They all delivered messages and did things that were instilled into us and made us the men that we became."

BRINGING THE VISION TO LIFE

"PR was the one with his own podcast before everyone had a podcast. It was like 'Hey, I'm about to get you guys on the podcast talking about whatever. When would be a great time?' I was like, the only time is usually when LeBron's in his haircut. He's like, yeah, okay, and we had some small talk about it.

"The Nike suite where LeBron gets his haircut, a lot of athletes come through there. I said, 'What if you catch them on your podcast while they're getting the haircut, kind of like a barbershop talk?' And we both talked more about it, like that would be crazy because the barbershop is always kind of a freestyle, like the conversations go all over the place and you don't necessarily have a topic unless somebody brings up something. PR's like, 'Great idea that we might tape it so then they can hear the clippers in the background.' We both said some of the best conversations come up in the barbershop.

"The [NBA] All-Star that year was in Toronto, so the conversation went from doing a podcast. So maybe we should just do an actual barbershop and have people come in, and we kind of host and talk to them and capture it on video while they're getting haircuts?

"So, the first 'pilot' took place in Toronto, and it was incredible. We had [radio personality] Ebro, and obviously he's a trained media guy. He kind of helped guide us editorially. That particular *Shop*, we had Ronnie Fieg. We had Future, José Bautista, Kevin Durant, James Harden. LeBron, Maverick, Steve Stoute came by, Rich [Paul] was there. And it was just literally the freest conversation, and we were like, we can do something with this.

"I think that's my part of being one of the creators. That is what my thing was. I wanted a place where it was comfortable for everybody, because everybody's comfortable in a barber's chair.

"Obviously, with Uninterrupted and SpringHill, we were so confident in the product that if nobody took to it, we could do it ourselves. We had already done it. And I think that's kind of the model for anything that you're passionate about.

THE SHOP PILOT SEASON, EPISODE 1, TORONTO, ON

“There was no script because the barbershop has no script.”

“We had the resources to film ourselves. So, we had the Toronto episode and the New Orleans episode. We didn’t have a vehicle. We didn’t have a YouTube, but we had something to present. We had a product to show, but we didn’t have that thought process of TV or whatever, we thought we would put it out on something, but we never thought we would be on HBO. You never think when you’re writing a book that it’s gonna be a movie, right?

“The New Orleans shop we had buttoned up because the Toronto one, we were all over the place. We had kind of a format of how we want to do things. And honestly, that was my last show that I personally was on. We had a mixture of the right guests and sort of a format of how to go forward. We didn’t have to pitch it to HBO, although if we had to go in and pitch it, we had something to show. We can show them this is what we want to build and take advice from them of how to make it better for TV. We could say, ‘This is what we want to do,’ and they can see it and say, ‘This is going to work.’”

WHAT MAKES *THE SHOP* DIFFERENT?

“There was no script because the barbershop has no script. *The Shop* has no script, still currently. No script. I mean, we have some things that we want to touch on with people or they may tell us ahead of time what they want to get out, say for instance Travis Scott has an album about to drop. Yeah, we’re gonna talk about it because he wants to get that out, but the revolving conversation in the room, it’s just very genuine. I mean, it’s as genuine as we’re talking about right now. I don’t have a script of what I’m about to tell you.

“One of the other things that was really important to me to do with *The Shop*: We know the people that we love and are fans of, but we love them for what they do. And I think that the show gives people the opportunity to see why you love the person.

“There’s certain people that, outside of music or sports, you’ve never really heard them talk, and you realize how smart they are when you hear them in a real conversation with other minds going, crisscrossing ideas.

“Think of a [Season 6 guest] Druski, right? Or one of these guys that has a persona where you always think, ‘He’s always just joking or this person is always so serious.’ In our show’s environment, these big-time athletes’ or celebs’ guard is down. I want people to see that. I want you to see the other side of just a guy that lines up every Sunday or a tennis player that you only see swing a racket. The other side, the intelligence side, the father side or . . . the husband side, or whatever that is. I wanted to create that. We wanted you to see *people*.”

THE SHOP'S LEGACY

“I’ll say we don’t do it to sell things. We do it because it’s authentic to what we’re about, and the selling part, the business side of it, comes secondary to the authenticity and who we are and what we stand for.”

"My barbershop experience started with my dad."

SEASON 6, EPISODE 1, PHOENIX, AZ

PERSONAL BARBERSHOP EXPERIENCES

"My barbershop experience started with my dad. It all started from my dad taking me. Even that is a rite of passage. If you have a dad, that's one of the first things. It's a big moment when you get to pick your own haircut. For the first two years, my dad picked my haircut, and I remember that moment I got to pick my own haircut. The real big one is when you get to pick your own barber.

"The barbers were very respected by everyone because they could talk about and relate to anything. Their conversation was about things like sports and what was going on in the neighborhood, but also, they could talk business and investments a bit. Back then, they were entrepreneurial when nobody else was. Barbers in my hood provided jobs, had to buy insurance, some of them owned the buildings that they operated out of.

"All the biggest dope boys in the hook got their hair cut. They would walk in with bankrolls of cash. People would have appointments, and they would buy off everybody that's waiting in line to cut in front. They'd actually say, 'I'm buying everybody haircut so I can go next.' That was a whole different experience.

"That idea, a lot of people with big personalities, all laughing and joking and bouncing back and forth between kind of serious conversations, is how I grew up my whole life."

BRINGING THE VISION TO LIFE

"Making any show is hard. They always present different reasons, but I mean, every episode still is an adventure.

"There was a guy who was running HBO Sports at the time named Peter Nelson. He was a visionary at HBO Sports who saw the show on YouTube. He was like, 'This is an HBO show.' We never pitched it. Nothing, that was his call. That was totally his idea. Peter also said, 'I will only greenlight the show if Mav is on it.' I never even saw myself as doing that. Didn't want to do it, zero interest in it. I don't even like seeing myself or hearing my voice.

"*The Shop* is not an interview show. It's a barbershop conversation. It's not like you walk in the barbershop and go, 'Let's talk to you today!' and ask you 20 questions. It's thrown around; the subject changes fast. We want to keep that structure in our format, which is authentic to *The Shop*. It's enjoyable for the guest and it's what consumers are showing up to see.

"The people who come on the show I'm naturally curious about when you see me on the show. The editors obviously do an amazing job at making me look good, but those questions I ask are just things I genuinely want to know. I genuinely want to know that about them. Those aren't set questions or anything. I genuinely want to understand those people."

WHAT MAKES *THE SHOP* DIFFERENT?

"The first time someone says something really, I can always feel the moment on the episode when the ice gets broken. It's either somebody curses, sometimes that's it; somebody says something really personal, and everyone is like, 'OK, that's what we're doing.' Sometimes it's minute one. Sometimes it takes 20 minutes, but I can always see.

"The hardest part is scheduling. They all have 17 people who work for them because they're all running around doing a billion other things. Imagine trying to get all those schedules to line up.

"The second hardest part is now you got them all there. Making sure they all get that moment in the conversation, because the audience wants to hear from them. That's why they're on the show. They came to the show to speak about their thing, and they're excited because once they're there, they see people opening up. Gotta make sure everybody has their moment. Then there's certain things just that come with making any show. How can you keep the audience's attention? Why should the audience give a fuck about this show? Why should they keep coming back for more? That's every show. Not overly particular to ours.

"We do a rolling start when we tape. Jay-Z, during his episode, leaned over to Paul and was like 'Yo Mav, PR!' We were 25 or 30 minutes into cameras rolling. He was like, 'Have we started?' And PR was like, 'We started 30 minutes ago.' He's like 'Shit!,' so that rolling start also allows people to just be comfortable."

THE SHOP'S LEGACY

"I'm not wanting to pat myself, or ourselves the company, on the back, but I think—listen, we weren't the first show to have a conversation, and lots of shows doing that before us. I do think our company, Uninterrupted, definitely led to athletes going, 'This is something I want to do.' Storytelling in a way that we didn't have when I grew up."

"I want *The Shop* to be known as the show that became a brand that was really bringing people of all different walks of life together to discuss topics. Of which they both agree and disagree but are willing to listen to both sides.

"You're welcome to come in here but may not be ready for it but listen to and understand conversation that goes many different ways that you may agree with. You may not even be ready to hear it because you may not be ready to make that change, but you're welcome inside here. No matter what, you're welcome to listen and also express yourself, too."

> "I want people to look at *The Shop* and see a reflection of themselves in their community…"

SEASON 4, EPISODE 3, MIAMI, FL

YOU KNOW

DON'T TAKE IT PERSONAL?

IT'S HARD NOT TO.

HOW PEOPLE
SAY,

WE'RE HUMAN
BEINGS, RIGHT?

Historically, athletes have been encouraged to focus solely on their sport, with their opinions on non-sporting matters often relegated to the sidelines. However, in today's sports world, the voices of athletes resonate far beyond the confines of courts and fields. *The Shop* exemplifies this shift. Before the advent of such platforms, prominent athletes rarely had the opportunity to candidly express themselves outside their sports.

SEASON 1, EPISODE 2, WASHINGTON, DC

"This format has allowed athletes to be seen not just as sports figures but as multifaceted individuals with insights and opinions that extend far beyond their professional achievements."

In an unfiltered, barbershop-style setting, *The Shop* disrupts this norm by providing a haven where athletes can express themselves without the constraints of sports-centric interviews. It's not about the next game or the last play; it's about them as individuals, their life experiences, and their perspectives on a variety of topics. This format has allowed athletes to be seen not just as sports figures but as multifaceted individuals with insights and opinions that extend far beyond their professional achievements.

Athletes on the show often discuss personal struggles, challenges with mental health, and the impact of fame on their personal lives. These conversations are pivotal, as they debunk the myth of the invincible athlete, showing that strength also lies in openness and honesty. The relaxed environment encourages open dialogue, often leading to profound insights and unexpected revelations. This atmosphere, devoid of press conference formalities or post-game interview clichés, allows for a more nuanced exploration of issues, both personal and professional.

Transitioning from the realm of personal journeys and societal reflections shared by athletes on *The Shop*, we pivot to the core of their professional lives—their excellence on the field. This shift takes us from the deeply personal insights into the athletes' lives off the field to the determination, skill, and relentless pursuit of greatness that define their on-field performance. It's a journey from understanding the person behind the athlete to celebrating the achievements and the sheer dedication it takes to excel in the competitive world of sports.

“For us as athletes, it’s the longest, shortest thing that we can do in our life to get the maximum out of it. If you lose the joy of the craft that you’re in, then you’re going to cheat the game and you’re gonna cheat yourself and then ultimately you’re gonna cheat your loved ones.

“And that’s why I’m still doing what I’m doing, because I want to continue to inspire not only the people in my household, but everybody that I can while I can. I want people to say, ‘This motherfucker is the greatest I’ve ever seen.’”

SEASON 4, EPISODE 1, LOS ANGELES, CA

“I really feel like a zoo animal . . . Like I got people who say, ‘Odell, dance!’ like I’m a show monkey or something. Like I’m a puppet. You know what I mean? That doesn’t feel good but it’s like damn, can you ever really detach from that?”

ODELL BECKHAM JR.
SEASON 1, EPISODE 1, LOS ANGELES, CA

"I can still remember it. When I was 19 and I declared for the draft, I had $151 in my bank account as a college student. I declared for the draft, got an agent. The agent offered me a hundred thousand to help with expenses upfront. Luckily, I had two parents who said, 'That's too damn much.' But they were cool with me getting $25,000. So you know what happened? I was at Wake Forest in Winston. I went to the bank right up the street so I could see what the statement looked like. I went and got the statement. That shit said, $25,151 [Laughs]."

CHRIS PAUL
SEASON 6, EPISODE 8, LOS ANGELES, CA

the
truth

"What a lot of people don't know is when you go in there, you be so tunnel vision. You don't have time to think about nobody. Your family, the crowd—none of that. You're just thinking about somebody punching at you, and you want to win. That's all you can think about is the game plan. What you got to do, and to win."

"I also feel like I'm the best as well. So I don't even think about losing. But I know that it's possible. When you go in there, you take that risk. But I'm willing to risk it all to win big. I'm betting on myself every time, no matter who it is. I'm willing to go in there and test my skills."

DEVIN HANEY
SEASON 6, EPISODE 6, LOS ANGELES, CA

"A lot of guys come in the game and just cruise through once they get that little paycheck. You know, it's like, do you really value this? I remember days playing outside, holes in a show, going hard. Not making a dollar from it. There's a few guys that take that same approach in the league. Like that."

DEMAR DEROZAN
SEASON 2, EPISODE 4,
LOS ANGELES, CA

“Wrecks are going to happen.”

BUBBA WALLACE
ON NOT HAVING FEAR
SEASON 4, EPISODE 6, LOS ANGELES, CA

ELENA DELLE DONNE
SEASON 1, EPISODE 2, WASHINGTON, DC

"I ignore the trolls. But it's like what's going on in here? [points to head] That's huge. There's nobody who talks to you in a day more than yourself. Think about that little voice in your head that's like, ba-ba, ba-ba, ba-ba. It's like, shut up."

"We have to fight these battles so hopefully, you know, your daughter won't have to."

SEASON 1, EPISODE 2, WASHINGTON, DC

“I was talking to somebody the other day and they were saying how athletes are so interesting because they could be one way in their field of sport and then off the court, they could be a totally different human being.”

VICTOR OLADIPO
SEASON 1, EPISODE 2, WASHINGTON, DC

TOM BRADY
SEASON 4, EPISODE 2, LOS ANGELES, CA

"I can really just be the best with the body that I was given, you know. You know there's certain things that I certainly cannot do. And I have the awareness to realize okay I can't do those things. You can't do everyone else's job. I can't block, tackle, run, catch . . . sure as hell can't run. But I can throw the shit out of a ball, you know, so let me just do that."

“You started playing because it was fun. And then you get to this pinnacle and it’s no longer fun.”

DRAYMOND GREEN
SEASON 5, EPISODE 7, PORTLAND, OR

"Confidence for me stems all the way back to my mom. The way she supported me gave me the ultimate confidence to go out and pretty much say fuck everybody. Because I always viewed it as I got a much better chance at being me, and either you're going to love it or hate it but you're going to have an opinion about it one way or another. And so for me, whether you think I'm good or bad, I did my job because you not stuck here trying to figure it out, you made your decision. I fucking made you make that decision though. You didn't just make it on your own."

KITH

“Only by admitting who you are do you get what you want. I played all my cards, and this is what you get . . . I thought, I don’t want anybody else to tell my story.”

KEVIN LOVE
SEASON 4, EPISODE 5, NEW YORK CITY, NY

"My dad was my biggest supporter and he's probably the reason why I had the career that I had. But the first time that he turned around to me and said, 'you did good' was when I won my 100th cap for playing for my country."

DAVID BECKHAM
SEASON 4, EPISODE 6, LOS ANGELES, CA

“In order to win,
you gotta do everything right.”

CARMELO ANTHONY
SEASON 4, EPISODE 4, NEW YORK CITY, NY

A'JA WILSON
SEASON 5, EPISODE 2, CLEVELAND, OH

"I wanted to be different. I want it to be something that's like, I want to change it. I want to break that glass ceiling."

"If I'm not marketable, I'm nothing. I think that's our biggest barrier is we can be that best player. But if you're not marketable, if you don't look a certain way, sound a certain way, especially being a Black woman, I think our biggest thing would have to be sharing our stories."

“Man . . . standing on the mound, 50,000 people in the Bronx. And like, it don’t start until I’m ready. You know what I’m saying? I get goose bumps thinking about it now.”

CC SABATHIA
ON PLAYING FOR THE YANKEES
SEASON 2, EPISODE 5, LOS ANGELES, CA

SEASON 5, EPISODE 7, PORTLAND, OR

ON-FIELD MINDSET

"Why do what you do if you don't feel like you're the best? Or you're giving it your all? You know, you're not, you don't play basketball to be the second best of all time. You play to be the best of all time. And you've got to say, I want to be the MVP. And it's only going to make the team better because sports and football is a team sport. So, you know, you play with that chip, that chip on your shoulder, I feel like it's only helping everybody. But for me, you know, I always, I'm going to say I'm the best, man. Even if I've got one leg out there and can't catch nothing."

DEANDRE HOPKINS
SEASON 2, EPISODE 2,
LOS ANGELES, CA

"Since I've been in the league, defense has been changing. Like they don't play me how they play other quarterbacks and stuff. So I gotta get ready for a dogfight every game. They gonna play they best. Being honest, I really can care less. Like I'm going out there to just try to win. Yeah, I'm locked in. I don't really care what the people gonna say. 'Cause they going to say whatever. Win or lose regardless."

"I gotta get the dub for our fans. That's why I'm locked in. I'm gonna have them sad while we over here celebrating because our fans, our fans actually DM us and be like, oh, we can't let the Steelers win. They say, my best friend's a Steelers fan, this and that. So definitely I wanna make them happy."

LAMAR JACKSON
SEASON 5, EPISODE 1, LOS ANGELES, CA

Shave

“That’s my mentality. I’ve always been doubted. Everybody said a lot about me and it’s, I’ve always understood that my game can do the most talking. So, everybody can say whatever they want and the whole crowd can do whatever but my game’s ultimately going to prove itself. And so, at the end that’s just kind of why I’ve, I mean, I just let all the emotions out and everything and every game is just because of that.”

TRAE YOUNG
SEASON 3, EPISODE 1,
CHICAGO, IL

“One of my mottos is, ‘Be where my feet at.’ Straight up. I’m not worried about the future. I’m not worried about the past. Let me do this drill 100 percent perfectly. So, then the next time I do it, it’s easier, you know what I’m saying.”

CHASE YOUNG
SEASON 4, EPISODE 3, MIAMI, FL

BB
BALENCIAGA

"Here's how I think about losing: A lot of it is framing.

"There's this misconception that people who are successful at their craft are just more talented than everyone else, that they win all the time. But the reality is you win only because you have lost more than most can endure. You have high risk aggression. You've put yourself in more situations where you have failed and lost so you build resilience. Those who win, lose. And while our winning is what's celebrated, our growth comes from our losses tenfold, man."

PAUL RABIL
SEASON 5, EPISODE 6, NEW YORK CITY, NY

PEOPLE ASK WHAT'S THE SECRET.

Steve Stoute

SEASON 5, EPISODE 2, CLEVELAND, OH

I DON'T SLEEP MUCH

AND I DON'T SEE MY FAMILY MUCH.

THAT'S THE SECRET.

"The Black barbershop stands as a testament to the power of hustle."

In *The Shop*, hustle isn't a buzzword. Hustle isn't a cheesy brand strategy slapped on workout T-shirts and avocado-based protein powders. What the majority considers hustle now isn't what we're discussing here. When we talk about hustle, we talk about the entrepreneurial spirit that for generations has made this nation a beacon for those wishing to come here to find their fortunes. Hustle isn't a social media account; it's a very real way of life for many of us, especially those who balance multiple factors like a successful career and family.

The Black barbershop stands as a testament to the power of hustle. It showcases how a space can evolve to serve multiple purposes—a grooming parlor, a networking hub, a marketplace, and a cultural center. In doing so, it underscores the role of small businesses in driving economic empowerment and social cohesion within communities.

Many Black barbershops started as modest ventures but have grown into cornerstone establishments within their neighborhoods. The owners, often revered figures in the community, provide haircuts, mentorship, and guidance, particularly to younger patrons. They create employment opportunities, train apprentices, and, in many cases, help spark a passion for entrepreneurship in others. Their shops become more than businesses; they're incubators for economic growth and self-sufficiency within the Black community.

Patrons of these establishments mirror this entrepreneurial drive. The barbershop often serves as a melting pot of local businessmen, aspiring artists, and other community figures, all sharing a unified hustle mentality. These spaces foster a unique form of networking, where connections are made, business ideas are exchanged, and entrepreneurial seeds are sown, often between the buzz of clippers and the casual chatter of the day.

In many Black barbershops, the entrepreneurial spirit extends beyond the core business of haircuts. It's not unusual to find a variety of goods for sale—from homemade food items to the latest electronics.

SEASON 5, EPISODE 7, PORTLAND, OR

SEASON 5, EPISODE 7, PORTLAND, OR

This entrepreneurial ethos is not just about making money; it's about creating and sustaining a vibrant community ecosystem. It's about leveraging every opportunity—be it selling products or engaging in friendly wagers—to foster a sense of agency and self-reliance. The hustle mentality found in these spaces is more than a means to an end; it's a celebration of the entrepreneurial spirit that has been a key driver of progress and resilience in the African American community.

In the unique setting of *The Shop*, where the raw authenticity of a barbershop converges with the glitz of celebrity culture, a diverse array of guests have taken the chair, each bringing their own brand of business acumen, built off 100 percent hustle. This eclectic mix mirrors the real-life dynamics of a barbershop, where people from all walks of life come together, united by the universal pursuit of success.

Guests like Rich Paul, a powerhouse in the sports management world, exemplify the hustle required to make it in America. His journey from selling vintage jerseys out of his trunk to representing some of the biggest names in sports is a testament to his savvy and determination. Paul's story resonates deeply in *The Shop*, symbolizing how vision and grit can propel one from humble beginnings to the pinnacle of professional success.

Or take someone like Jake Paul, a controversial figure yet

a successful entrepreneur in his own right, who represents a newer wave of business savvy. Leveraging his social media fame, Paul has demonstrated how today's digital landscape offers unconventional paths to success. His presence in *The Shop* highlights how the definition of a business leader is ever-evolving, shaped by the opportunities and challenges of the digital age.

The show also gives insight into the brains of people like Steve Stoute, a music executive turned marketing legend who epitomizes the entrepreneurial spirit that drives American business. His transition from the music industry to founding Translation, a successful marketing agency, and UnitedMasters, a platform for independent artists, underscores the versatility and adaptability needed in today's business landscape. Stoute's narrative is a powerful reminder that success often requires the courage to innovate and venture into uncharted territories.

The Shop not only offers a window into the minds of these successful figures but also serves as an allegory for the diversity of customers in a barbershop. *The Shop* showcases how successful businesspeople can emerge from any circumstance. It's a reminder that in America, the hustle to succeed knows no bounds and that the path to success is as varied as those who walk through a barbershop's doors.

SEASON 5, EPISODE 7, PORTLAND, OR

FAT JOE
SEASON 5, EPISODE 4, NEW YORK CITY, NY

“I’m a hustler who converted to a rapper. I chose rap. If I had a choice, I would be an R&B singer. If I could trade it right now? My whole career of rap for an R&B career? I would get on my knees, throw roses at the girls and do all of that.”

"I felt like, okay, this is a responsibility I have to put Black culture on mainstream television. I felt so proud. Because it wasn't corny. Because it was truthful."

STEVE STOUTE
SEASON 5, EPISODE 2, CLEVELAND, OH

"What our kids don't understand is how hard it is to be successful. That's the only thing. It's hard to be successful. So, if you want to be a rapper or you want to be a comedian?

Well, are you willing to commit to the years and years and years of not being successful?"

RICH PAUL
SEASON 6, EPISODE 2, SALT LAKE CITY, UT

"I told my mother I wanted to be an actor. And she said, 'You know that's a really hard business to get into.' I told her, 'Either I make it in that or I don't make it at all.'"

MARTIN LAWRENCE
SEASON 2, EPISODE 5, LOS ANGELES, CA

"I never was cool with being second. Yeah. I don't know what second place feel like. You can call it cocky, whatever the fuck you want, but I just don't like being in second place. And sometimes I feel like I have to reinvent myself because I didn't feel back to second place. And it's not because it is what it is. It is what it ain't. It's like you're not that young rapper no more. You're not that young fly MC. But I still can pull a move on you motherfuckers real quick."

SNOOP DOGG
SEASON 1, EPISODE 1,
LOS ANGELES, CA

adidas

FRESH
ERS

LOWERS
KLUTCH

RICH PAUL

In this chapter, we delve into the concept of hustle—a theme as integral to success in business as it is in personal growth. At the forefront of translating hustle into tangible success is Rich Paul, a renowned sports agent, and a master of maneuvering within the high-stakes world of sports management. His trajectory from selling vintage jerseys out of the trunk of his car to representing some of the biggest names in sports exemplifies the very essence of hustle that *The Shop* seeks to explore.

As Rich Paul joins us in this conversation, we're not just anticipating insights into the sports industry; we're tapping into the mindset and strategies that define a hustler in the truest sense.

SEASON 6, EPISODE 2, SALT LAKE CITY, UT

“For me, it’s always been hustle.”

ON THE ORIGINS OF HIS HUSTLE:
“I was kind of born into being an entrepreneur. My community was that everybody that I grew up with had a hustle, and a job. Very little careers but multiple hustles and multiple jobs, and so I don’t know anything different.

“I might have been nine years old when I realized that everything we did growing up was literally a hustle, and so I wanted to be good at everything. I was never a little kid playing a card game for the fun of it. Even at my company retreats, I can’t just play cards. And I never played video games because if I couldn’t gamble in it and be really good at it to win, I didn’t do it. Bowling, horseshoes, pitching quarters, darts, racing, ping-pong, anything that you can bet, I was good at it. That’s how it was.”

ON HIS RELATIONSHIP WITH THE BARBERSHOP GROWING UP:
“My barbershop experience was a little different, because we really had to be careful of what barbershops we went to and where that barbershop was located. You can be in that chair and the wrong person walks in that barbershop, and now it’s an issue. The best barbers might cut hair in a place that wasn’t your comfort zone. And so, you always had to be, no pun intended, sharp.

“Any conversation that gives someone insight to further themselves is important. And I think that the whole idea of *The Shop*, and the whole idea of barbershops itself, is that you’re turning what could be a haircut into an education.”

ON HIS DISTINCTIVE HUSTLE:
“I’m working to be impactful or I’m in a disruptive perspective. Those are the two lanes I drive in. I don’t drive the shoulder or the highway.

“I don’t really do busy work.

“It is so important to be aware. I couldn’t leave the house without being aware. So, I carry it with me. Self-awareness comes standard.

“For me, it’s always been hustle. And that’s how I got here when I was selling jerseys at the back of my trunk. It was because I realized that. These jerseys that I was selling didn’t exist in my city and I didn’t sit back and wait for them to get there. I went and got them and brought them there. and I think oftentimes people want to be in a different space than what they’re actually in. But they don’t really jump the hurdles necessary to win that race, if that makes sense.

“It’s hard for me to see somebody be really successful at something and not really care to take it all the way there. It’s a struggle for me. No matter how much money you got. I don’t know. It’s a weird thing when I’m always just in grind mode.”

ON BUILDING A HUSTLE, COMMUNITY, AND THE LEGACY HE WANTS TO LEAVE:
“I’ve always been someone that’s been connected to culture. Throughout the ecosystem, whether it’s been fashion, music, sports, community, or business.

“I talk to my kids about just getting awareness through dialogue, through paying attention to detail. I talk to my son, ‘Did you see that? Why he did that?’ That’s important because he didn’t grow up like me. Even though he’s growing up a lot differently than I did, I still want him to be equipped with those attributes.

“Everybody’s gonna have an opinion. Everybody’s gonna have a different perspective. That’s why *The Shop* is good. You got young men and women, everyone has a different experience with things. There's narratives. There's people with agendas.

"My drive within my hustle has not changed at all. What I'm hustling for and why I'm hustling has changed a lot. Completely yeah, I have the same motivation, that same get up and go as I had when I was in my environment growing up. The difference is the stakes are much higher. The why I'm hustling is definitely different."

ON THE VALUE OF *THE SHOP* AS A PLATFORM FOR ATHLETES: "The platform is important for the athlete because It's a 24-hour, 365 news cycle today in sports. It wasn't always like that. But today it is. And there are narratives. There are people with agendas. There's this perception of things and how it went, but you need to hear from the horse's mouth sometimes. If that person is coming from a place of truth and it's authentic, you can tell. And that's why I think *The Shop* does a great job of giving these men and women platforms, by putting a balanced and diversified group together to be able to allow the conversation to have some depth to it."

SEASON 2, EPISODE 4, LOS ANGELES, CA

FOR WHAT

YOU

A RESPONSIBILITY TO SPEAK UP

BELIEVE IN.

Michael Bennett

SEASON 1, EPISODE 1, LOS ANGELES, CA

Historically, the barbershop has been more than a place to get a fresh cut; community, culture, and conversations converge. These spaces' profound role in Black America's social and political fabric cannot be overstated. Once barbershops became community hubs, it was an obvious conclusion that these spaces would facilitate dialogue about civil rights and social justice. Barbershops were safe havens where Black Americans could share their experiences and strategies for combating racial injustice away from the prying eyes of a segregated society. Like churches, they served as informal meeting places for community groups where activists could plan.

LARGE BARBERSHOP IN HARLEM, CIRCA 1929

These discussions often led to significant community actions that played a crucial role in the fight for desegregation and voting rights. The barbershop was where the grassroots met the razor's edge, cutting through societal norms to question and challenge the status quo. These establishments served as symbols of unity and resilience in the face of systemic oppression.

The barbershop has become a site for bridging generational divides within the African American community.

It's a place where the elders' wisdom meets the youth's energy. Older generations share stories and lessons from past struggles for civil rights and equality, whereas younger patrons bring new perspectives and strategies for dealing with contemporary social issues. This intergenerational exchange enriches the community's understanding of social justice and strengthens its resolve to continue the fight for equity and inclusion.

The intergenerational discourse thriving in the barbershop finds a new platform in *The Shop*. The show amplifies this cross-generational exchange. Athletes and public figures from various backgrounds share their experiences with social issues, bridging the gap between the civil rights struggles of the past and the ongoing fight for equity, ensuring that these crucial conversations continue to resonate and evolve in our digital age.

An essential theme in *The Shop* is the intersection of sports and social issues. By intertwining the two worlds, *The Shop* echoes the barbershop's role as a community forum, evolving the conversation to include broader audiences and challenging the traditional limitations on athletes' voices. Athletes on the show often discuss how their status can be leveraged to effect change. Conversations delve into topics like racial inequality, police brutality, and political activism, offering a perspective often missing in traditional sports media. These discussions underscore the importance of athletes as voices in the broader societal conversation, challenging the outdated notion that they should "stick to sports."

Sports figures like Malcolm Jenkins and Bubba Wallace bring a unique perspective to *The Shop*. Their experiences highlight the intersection of sports with social activism, echoing broader conversations about race, identity, and the role of athletes in advocating for change. Their stories underscore the challenges and responsibilities of being a Black athlete in the spotlight, navigating their profession and activism.

Conversations with cultural commentators and entertainers like Killer Mike and Jemele Hill add another layer to the discourse, bridging the gap between entertainment, culture, and social issues. Their contributions emphasize the role of media and entertainment in shaping public opinion and driving social change.

The candid and often deep discussions on *The Shop* reflect the shifting landscape of athlete and celebrity engagement in issues. The show moves beyond traditional sports commentary and celebrity interviews, delving into the heart of societal challenges and personal experiences. It creates a space where guests can share their journeys, struggles, and viewpoints, fostering a more profound understanding among viewers.

The Shop demystifies celebrity by fostering candid conversations that reveal the human side of fame. In the laid-back atmosphere of a barbershop, stars and athletes candidly discuss issues close to their hearts, from personal struggles to broader societal matters. As guests share personal stories and opinions, the show peels back the veneer of celebrity, allowing viewers to connect with the individual behind the notoriety. The show's power lies in its ability to humanize these individuals, presenting them not as distant celebrities but as real people with real stories to tell.

Including guests like Stacey Abrams and Governor Gavin Newsom signifies the show's commitment to discussing political activism and civic engagement. Their appearances allow for deep discussions about voting rights, political representation, and the challenges African Americans face in the political arena. These dialogues provide invaluable insights into the workings of democracy and the importance of political participation.

Today, the barbershop's role has evolved again. Now, they're not just talking about change; they're driving it. From hosting voter registration drives to serving as venues for health awareness campaigns, these spaces have become pivotal in addressing issues that disproportionately impact the Black community. Conversations about police brutality, systemic racism, and political disenfranchisement

SEASON 2, EPISODE 6, NEW YORK CITY, NY

are as every day as those about sports and local news. These dialogues often highlight the barbershop's role in shaping not just hairstyles but also societal attitudes and actions.

Similarly, *The Shop* has evolved as a platform, going from being a platform where news-making headlines are discussed to becoming a newsmaker of its own accord.

> "Conversations about police brutality, systemic racism, and political disenfranchisement are as every day as those about sports and local news."

A fantastic illustration of this point was in Season 2 when California Governor Gavin Newsom joined LeBron James and former college athletes on a momentous occasion: the signing of SB 206, known as the Fair Pay to Play Act. This act, a pioneering piece of legislation in the United States, allows student athletes in California to receive compensation for using their name, image, and likeness. The signing of SB 206 on *The Shop* represented more than just a legislative victory; it symbolized a significant shift in the conversation about the rights and compensation of student athletes. The debate around compensating college athletes, particularly in revenue-generating sports like basketball and football, has been contentious for years. By signing the bill in the company of LeBron James, a vocal advocate for athlete compensation, and on a platform known for its candid discussions, Governor Newsom brought national attention to a critical issue.

This moment in *The Shop* ties into the broader narrative of the show as a space where influential figures can address pressing social justice topics. The act of signing SB 206 in such a public and influential forum highlights the show's commitment to discussing change and being an active participant in it.

SEASON 2, EPISODE 4, LOS ANGELES, CA

2019
Governor

WHILE THE VIBE IN *THE SHOP* IS ALWAYS POSITIVE AND EASYGOING, THERE ARE TIMES WHEN SERIOUS CONVERSATIONS NEED TO BE HAD.

FROM DISCUSSIONS AROUND OUR POLITICAL CLIMATE TO THE POWER AND IMPORTANCE OF VOTING TO A ONCE-IN-A-LIFETIME MOMENT WHERE THE SHOW MADE HISTORY, *THE SHOP* IS WHERE IMPORTANT DISCUSSIONS TAKE PLACE.

SEASON 2, EPISODE 4, LOS ANGELES, CA

"[Voter suppression] is the most serious thing facing our country today. Because there's nothing we want as a society that we can have without voting.

STACEY ABRAMS
SEASON 2, EPISODE 6, NEW YORK CITY, NY

MALCOLM JENKINS, ON THE HISTORIC NFL PROTESTS AGAINST POLICE BRUTALITY SEASON 2, EPISODE 6, NEW YORK CITY, NY

"So you basically had, you know, Colin, take a knee. And that sparked this national, really global, conversation about, you know, race, sports, and all these different things. And so what that did is we started a league-wide conversation amongst players and started to like organize with that.

"How do we take this from just a protest and actually like bring some action to it? All of a sudden, we started putting our voices together, and things started taking off.

"And so, the league came to us and said, well, okay, we see what you guys are doing. You're doing a bunch of work. Things that, that athletes really have never done before. And they said, you know, how do we, they wanted to know what we were doing. And we said, 'Look, just to let you know, we don't need your permission for anything. This is what we're going to do. If you want to support us . . .'

"There's the reason that we all started this, which is to effectuate change in our own communities and be able to support the work that needs to be done. What we've been able to do with the funds that we've secured from the league, guys have been able to really take over their own cities. Now you've got guys in Boston, and LA, and Baltimore, Philly, Louisiana, all these different things that are doing like phenomenal work. That are changing laws, lobbying for policy. We've never seen that kind of organization that has been player driven . . . but then now the league is blackballing Kaep."

"Certain things happen, things change in your life. Me having my own kids and then seeing the Trayvon Martin thing, it hit home. At the time, I think my oldest son was nine and my youngest son was six. I can't imagine if I sent my kid out and he didn't return home like that. So that's why I started thinking, if I can get 25,000 people to show up to a basketball game, I can reach so many more platforms when I talk."

LEBRON JAMES
SEASON 5, EPISODE 4, NEW YORK CITY, NY

OAMC

“You have a responsibility to speak up for what you believe in. When it comes to the real social issues of people of color . . . So when I was growing up, I was looking for Michael Jordan to say something, he never did. But now kids can look up and be like, what is LeBron saying?”

MICHAEL BENNETT
SEASON 1, EPISODE 1, LOS ANGELES, CA

"Ultimately, this NCAA model is going to fail. Their argument that people enjoy it more because we know you're not getting paid was always whack. No, I don't really. That has nothing to do with my enjoyment. But there's no way you should have coaches making eight, nine, or ten million dollars a year off your back and you get nothing out of it."

JEMELE HILL
SEASON 4, EPISODE 3,
MIAMI, FL

"You're challenging a system that's been entrenched in money, in power, and a certain way of thinking for a long time. A couple months ago, I had a good friend on campus, she goes to the student union, takes a picture. Who do they have hanging up there? Number Three jersey. Me. Number Ten jersey. Sue [Bird]. Fifty, [Rebecca] Lobo. I graduated in 2004. I mean we're talking about ten years later and they're still making money off of us."

DIANA TAURASI
SEASON 2, EPISODE 4, LOS ANGELES, CA

LAPSTONE

THE SHOP MADE LITERAL HISTORY IN SEASON 2. IN EPISODE 4, CALIFORNIA GOVERNOR GAVIN NEWSOM SIGNED THE FAIR PLAY TO PAY ACT, WHICH MADE CALIFORNIA THE FIRST STATE IN THE NATION TO ALLOW STUDENT ATHLETES TO RECEIVE COMPENSATION FROM THE USE OF THEIR NAME, IMAGE, AND LIKENESS.

SEASON 2, EPISODE 4, LOS ANGELES, CA

SEASON 2, EPISODE 4, LOS ANGELES, CA

MORE THAN AN ATHLETE

"... they're a little panicked. Because they recognize they're vulnerable. The gig's up."

GOVERNOR GAVIN NEWSOM
SEASON 2, EPISODE 4, LOS ANGELES, CA

"I've been getting calls from school presidents. They don't even outsource the phone calls out there. They all say, 'What the hell are you doing destroying college sports?' They all think this is the end of Title IX. They're saying, 'You're destroying the purity of amateurism.' I've gotten a few calls from Mark [Emmert, president of the NCAA]. He's trying to make sure I don't use this pen tonight. I mean look, they're a little panicked. Because they recognize they're vulnerable. The gig's up. Fourteen-plus billion dollars goes to these universities. A billion-plus revenue to the NCAA themselves. And the actual product, the folks that are putting their lives on the line, putting everything on the line are getting nothing."

I FEEL LIKE ONCE

THREE HUNDRED PEOPLE HAVE BOOED YOU, IT'S HARD TO FEEL NERVOUS.

Amber

SEASON 5, EPISODE 3, LOS AN

"... comedy, much like a classic barbershop, becomes the soul of community and connection."

Historically, African American humor has been a powerful tool for coping with and making sense of the complexities and injustices of life. In barbershops, humor becomes a communal language, a way to bond and to navigate the shared experiences of being Black in America.

Culturally, the barbershop as a comedy hub has been immortalized in various forms of media, most notably in film and television. Movies like the Barbershop series have popularized the image of the barbershop as a place of laughter and camaraderie, highlighting its role as a community center where humor is used to bridge generational and social gaps. These portrayals, though comedic, often carry deeper messages about community, identity, and social change.

Here we dive deep into the heart of laughter within *The Shop*. This isn't just about cracking jokes; it's about how comedy, much like a classic barbershop, becomes the soul of community and connection. In *The Shop*, humor does more than just elicit laughs—it bridges gaps, it tells truths, and it breaks down barriers.

In *The Shop*, comedy is more than a performance; it's a language, a way of finding common ground in a room full of diverse experiences and perspectives.

It's amazing how a well-timed joke can open the door to discussions about race, culture, and identity, or how a humorous anecdote can lead to real talk about the challenges and triumphs of life, isn't it? In *The Shop*, comedy becomes a tool, a way to ease into the tough stuff, making the hard-to-talk-about topics a little more approachable.

This chapter isn't just a rundown of the funniest moments in *The Shop*. It's an exploration of how humor in this unique setting often serves as a segue into deeper, more complex conversations. It's about understanding the role of laughter in building community and sparking conversation.

SEASON 2, EPISODE 4, LOS ANGELES, CA

“The funniest laugh is when you say the shit that motherfuckers ain’t supposed to say, that’s my job.”

JAMIE FOXX
SEASON 2, EPISODE 1, CHARLOTTE, NC

HERON

"It's this weird expectation for entertainers to be civil rights leaders, right? And then there's moments where it does overlap and there are very strong statements. Your life has become kind of this political statement in and of itself, right? So, there are times when it overlaps. And then, there are times where, if you're a comedian, if you're an actor, what you're doing is art. And what art is, is showing people your mistakes, showing people your flaws, showing people what's wrong. It shouldn't be beholden to this political obligation. And an entertainer being a role model is, it sometimes happens and sometimes they're just good at what they do."

JERROD CARMICHAEL
SEASON 2, EPISODE 1, CHARLOTTE, NC

“If I could do the exact same thing that I do and not be famous at all, I would fucking do that in a second. You know, I remember when I first started getting famous I was like, ‘I can’t do shrooms and walk around doing this.’ That was the first tangible thing fame took from me. My ability to publicly be on hallucinogens.”

SETH ROGEN
SEASON 2, EPISODE 2,
LOS ANGELES, CA

"Comedy has always been a major part of my life, which is why I don't miss an opportunity to work on my craft. I study myself and I study the greats. Growing up, I watched comedians like Eddie Murphy and Martin Lawrence and have had the privileges to work and tour with legends like Mike Epps; there was so much wisdom that was poured into me in that experience. It helped me so much and, reassured me that, I'm doing exactly what I'm supposed to be doing right now."

DESI BANKS
SEASON 6, EPISODE 1, PHOENIX, AZ

SEASON 2, EPISODE 2, LOS ANGELES, CA

ye
be Born
again

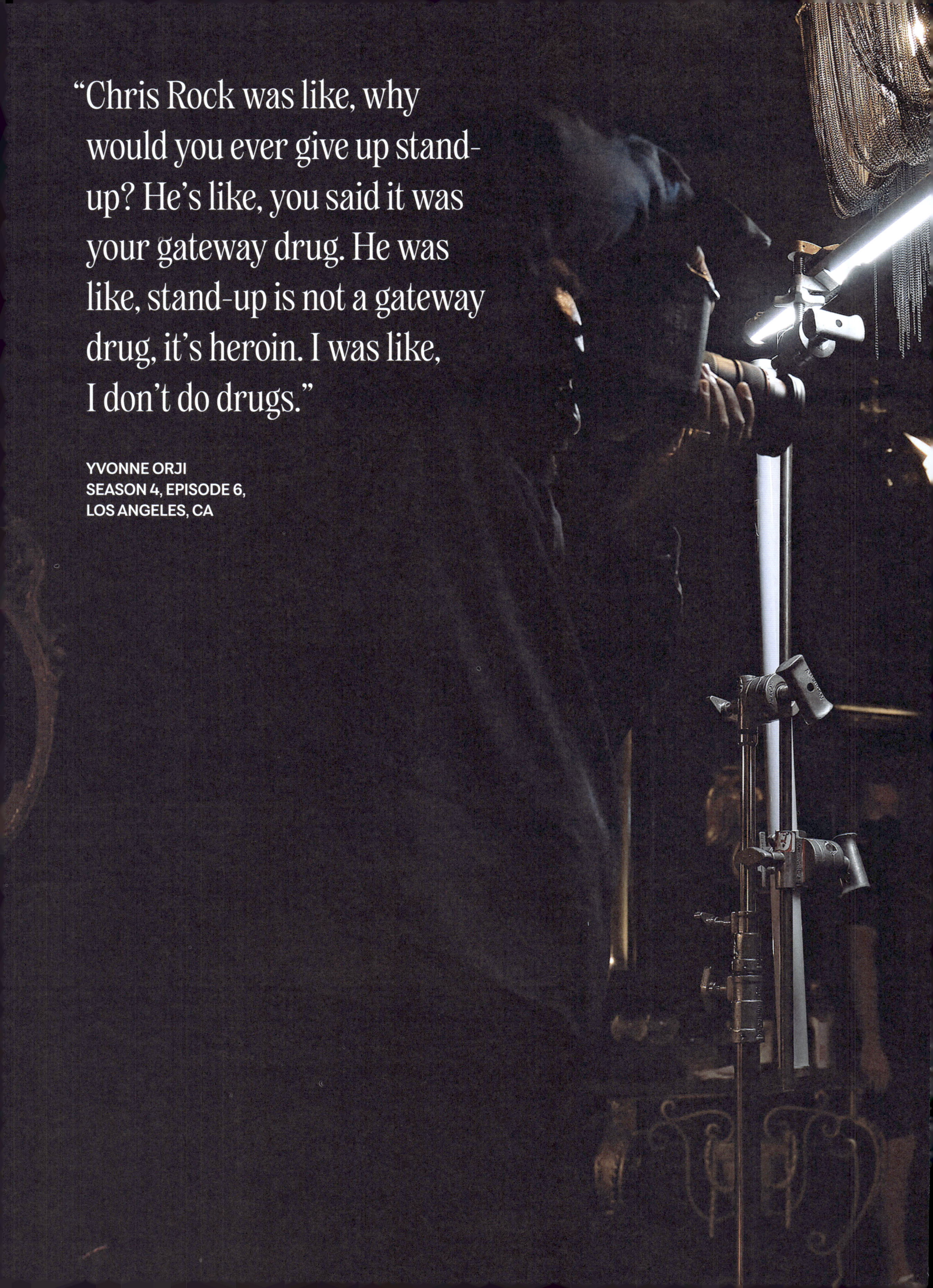

"Chris Rock was like, why would you ever give up stand-up? He's like, you said it was your gateway drug. He was like, stand-up is not a gateway drug, it's heroin. I was like, I don't do drugs."

YVONNE ORJI
SEASON 4, EPISODE 6,
LOS ANGELES, CA

THE POWER
OF A WOMAN

I JUST WANT

TO MAKE

MUSIC

AND CREATE.

Teyana Taylor

SEASON 6, EPISODE 4, LOS ANGELES, CA

> "In the cultural symphony *The Shop*, music plays more than just a background score—it's a vital, pulsating force that intertwines with the very essence of the show."

The role of music in barbershops is multifaceted. It's a conversation starter, a mood setter, and often, a bridge between generations. This dialogue fosters a deeper understanding and appreciation within the community and keeps the legacy of Black music alive and evolving. Who among us hasn't had a spirited debate about rap music in a barbershop?

In the cultural symphony *The Shop*, music plays more than just a background score—it's a vital, pulsating force that intertwines with the very essence of the show. This chapter explores how *The Shop* not only reflects but also amplifies the longstanding relationship between music and barbershops in the tapestry of culture. It's a journey into understanding how this intersection has shaped dialogues, influenced trends, and fostered a unique communal spirit.

In *The Shop*, music is a constant, dynamic presence. It's not just about having famous musicians as guests, but about delving into the deeper connections between their art and the wider world. The show has welcomed diverse musical artists, each sharing their unique stories, inspirations, and insights. These conversations reveal music's profound impact on personal identity, social movements, and cultural expressions.

Musicians discuss their creative processes, the challenges of the industry, and the responsibility that comes with having a platform. This provides an intimate glimpse into the artists' worlds and showcases the power of music as a tool for communication and change.

Moreover, *The Shop* highlights the symbiotic relationship between music and other cultural elements like fashion, language, and social activism. The discussions illustrate how music is intertwined with these aspects—influencing and being influenced by them. This reflects the barbershop's traditional role as a cultural melting pot, where different elements of community life blend harmoniously.

One of the most striking aspects of music's presence in *The Shop* is its role in bridging generational gaps. The show brings together artists from different eras, facilitating a rich exchange of ideas and experiences. Veteran musicians share the wisdom gained from years in the industry, while younger artists offer fresh perspectives and innovative approaches.

This intergenerational dialogue enriches the narrative, creating a tapestry of musical evolution and influence, making *The Shop* stand out as a vivid representation of the deep-seated bond between music and barbershops in culture.

SEASON 4, EPISODE 1, LOS ANGELES, CA

"Rap music is pugilism and poetry. The Star-Spangled Banner is a battle cry. If you listen to your national anthems from all over the world, if you listen to Celtic War songs, you read *The Iliad*, all of these things influence a certain masculinity. I think it's always needed in culture."

KILLER MIKE
SEASON 6, EPISODE 8, LOS ANGELES, CA

"I started writing it around that time. But I was like, I was anti kind of like what was going on because it was like, here is me and a picture of me in the projects that I grew up and the corner that I spent a lot of time on. And the songs are a reflection of what's really going on. There was nothing made up. It was just, even the name of the album comes from a guy who was like the big brother on the block named Illmatic, you know?"

NAS
SEASON 1, EPISODE 3,
LOS ANGELES, CA

"When I looked in the mirror, I knew
I had something to bring to the table.
So everything just started happening.
Like, you can feel that shit.

It's like a fucking game.

It's on fire.

You can feel it, you can feel it."

2 CHAINZ
SEASON 2, EPISODE 1,
CHARLOTTE, NC

“Since I was a little girl, I was working and the blessing in that is that my work was something that I actually did enjoy to do. And it was like okay, the love of it outweighs the stresses, and even now we all go through shit, and we all have problems, but it’s like when your love of something outweighs that, you’ll do anything to keep it going. So that’s truly been my heartbeat through it all and I was lucky that God blessed me with a sister that I got to go through it with.”

CHLOE BAILEY
SEASON 6, EPISODE 3, LOS ANGELES, CA

LA

BAD BUNNY
SEASON 4, EPISODE 1, LOS ANGELES, CA

"Es como si fueran cosas que siempre quise hacer de chamaquito pero quizas por la sociedad . . ."

"It's like if there were things I wanted to do since I was a little jit [slang for little kid], but maybe because of society, I didn't do it . . ."

"Como que, cabron, a veces me frustro. Parque muchas veces hay una presion, que a veses siento que es injusta."

"Like, motherfucker, sometimes I get frustrated because many times there is pressure, which sometimes I feel is unfair."

"I love the word grace. It's more so about like just knowing who you are and just doing what's comfortable for you and not letting people you know, pull you in 1,000 different directions because they, if you allowed, would have you doing all kind of stuff. It has to make sense for you. It can't make sense for them. And it can't be motivated by money."

JAY-Z
SEASON 4, EPISODE 1, LOS ANGELES, CA

"I love to perform and
I love to make music.

I don't like everything
that comes with it . . .

I just want to make
music and create."

TEYANA TAYLOR
SEASON 6, EPISODE 4, LOS ANGELES, CA

BABYFACE
SEASON 6, EPISODE 4, LOS ANGELES, CA

"The hardest thing is that when you're always chasing . . . when you're chasing yourself."

"I thrived on heartbreak, I thrived on pain that was in voices. When I first heard Toni Braxton, the pain that was in her voice. Mary J., the pain that she had. That gets me excited. Ooh, I can write for that. But through the pain and through the heartbreak, then there comes the other side of it and you do find love and that feeling. And so, a lot of times when I would write songs, I'd remember that pain that I felt as a kid and from the seventh and eighth grade. And I'd go to that place because it was so passionate that you feel that strongly than anytime in our life. And that's what I would use when I'm writing a song. I would go to that place.

"It's hard as an artist. It's hard to know when you're supposed to switch or not. And you also strive to always do something a little better, do something a little different. And it's hard to make that call because sometimes they make that change and it goes beyond. The hardest thing is that when you're always chasing . . . when you're chasing yourself. Michael Jackson spent a career chasing himself trying to beat *Thriller*."

JADAKISS
SEASON 4, EPISODE 5, NEW YORK CITY, NY

"We [his group The Lox] said when we signed our first deal, that none of this stuff that breaks other groups up . . . we wasn't going to let that intertwine us and you know, we been able to do good. No social media. If we have a gripe or discrepancy, we go behind closed doors and we iron it out. We leave it in there and we come out together."

Supreme
SPAGHETTI

ARTIST FEELS LIKE SUCH A DOUCHEY WORD

TO SAY.

Kenya Barris

SEASON 6, EPISODE 3, LOS ANGELES, CA

"... sanctuaries of storytelling, style, and art"

Barbershops are not just places for a haircut; they are sanctuaries of storytelling, style, and art. In the realm of film and television, the barbershop has been immortalized as a setting rich with narrative potential. It's depicted as a space where life's dramas unfold, a place of laughter, debate, and, sometimes, profound revelation. Movies like *Barbershop* and shows like *Atlanta* have used the barbershop as a backdrop, not just for its cultural significance, but for its artistic value—as a space where the stories of the African American community can be told with authenticity and depth.

This intersection of artistry and the barbershop setting within *The Shop* mirrors a larger cultural phenomenon where barbershops serve not just as places for grooming but as vibrant hubs of creativity and cultural exchange.

The show has hosted a wide range of artistic talents, from actors who share the intricacies of their craft and the emotional journey of embodying diverse characters to visual artists who discuss the inspirations behind their work and the messages they aim to convey. These conversations reveal the depth of thought, the passion, and the dedication that underpin artistic creation. They offer viewers insights into the creative process and the challenges and triumphs that accompany the life of an artist.

Moreover, *The Shop* has shone a spotlight on how artistry, whether in acting or visual art, serves as a medium for social commentary and change. Through their discussions, guests have explored how art can provoke thought, evoke emotion, and inspire action.

Through its candid discussions with actors, visual artists, and other creatives, the show has illuminated the myriad ways in which art intersects with and reflects our lives. As we reflect on these conversations, we are reminded of the enduring legacy of artists who use their platforms to challenge, celebrate, and change the world.

SEASON 7, EPISODE 4, LOS ANGELES, CA

SEASON 5, EPISODE 2, CLEVELAND, OH

ABOVE AND OPPOSITE: SEASON 7, EPISODE 4, LOS ANGELES, CA

“A microphone is more powerful than a grenade. I truly believe that. So, I’m never going to get in front of a microphone, and not have something impactful to say.”

“We’ve had a Black president of the United States, but we have never had a Black person run a major studio in Hollywood.”

“These images that we’re putting out. And sometimes they’re rough. Sometimes they’re fun. Sometimes it’s light. But we really do have the power to change the course of people’s lives, just by them seeing themselves on television and being not just seen in a positive light, but I always say just in the sunlight.”

LENA WAITHE
SEASON 1, EPISODE 3, LOS ANGELES, CA

"Comedy's a really interesting thing because it's the one thing that allows you to get a lesson but it's like taking medicine with a spoonful of sugar."

KENYA BARRIS
SEASON 6, EPISODE 3, LOS ANGELES, CA

"I like sitting at the bar, eating my crawfish watching the game. Like, it's just therapeutic. And people are just start, like, to crowd around me and I have no security. And like that was my issue at first. Like, I still feel hella normal. But I realize I can't be out in these streets like that because people will follow me. One time I had somebody follow me home!"

SAWEETIE
SEASON 4, EPISODE 6, LOS ANGELES, CA

"When you have the platform to speak,
when you've got the mic,
say what needs to be said."

ICE CUBE
SEASON 1, EPISODE 3, LOS ANGELES, CA

BOBBY HUNDREDS
SEASON 6, EPISODE 4, LOS ANGELES, CA

"If you don't see a place for yourself in the world, make one . . ."

"I wanted to be heard. I felt like I was excluded from every conversation. Nobody wanted to hear anything I had to say my entire life. . . . And I was just drawn to these marginal subcultures, these fringe interests like skateboarding and hardcore music and punk and backpack rap and graffiti. And there was no place for it in mainstream culture. So, I'm watching film, listening to music, and nobody's speaking my language. And then, it came to a point where I was like, 'Man, I just feel left out. I don't have my own community. But if I build a brand, I can create my own world.' So that's what I champion when I talk about entrepreneurialism and I'm inspiring young people to build brands or start off their careers. I'm like, 'If you don't see a place for yourself in the world, make one and then you can create a home for others to be welcomed, to be included in.' And it becomes a really beautiful and remarkable experience for everybody. And then, it inspires them to do the same. So, everybody wins."

"There's a lot of artists that make art for art's sake. They just make shit. Right? I'm going to make a pretty picture. It has no substance behind it. And for me, it's important that no matter what I do, it says something, because it has to hit here [points to heart]. So yeah, it's always that thing of me trying to outdo my last. But I don't get the feeling of no audience until it's a show. There's no instant gratification."

"At the time, man, you can't pronounce yourself as a creative, as a visual artist from a Black community in a lot of ways because you're looked down upon and there's words thrown at you, right? It wasn't as socially accepted as it is now. So for me, it was a thing that I always hid. And it wasn't until ... DJ Drama was my homie and we went to school together, and Drama would sell his mixtapes on the promenade, while I'm selling T-shirts that I've hand painted and stuff like that. But Drama was the first person that I knew within my circle that actually started making a little coin and bought the first painting I ever made."

HEBRU BRANTLEY
SEASON 6, EPISODE 5, LOS ANGELES, CA

“The thing about acting is that it’s truly, literally replicating things that people go through every single day. So, when someone’s screaming and shouting in the middle of an argument, you’re doing it. If your gut doesn’t feel like that, it doesn’t quite connect as actors.”

IDRIS ELBA
SEASON 5, EPISODE 6, NEW YORK CITY, NY

YOU'VE

EXFOLIATE

LIKE

A

FUCKING

GOT TO

MADMAN.

Pharrell Williams

SEASON 2, EPISODE 2, LOS ANGELES, CA

As we turn the pages to the final chapter of our journey through *The Shop*, we find ourselves reflecting on the profound insights and memorable quotes that have resonated within the walls of this groundbreaking show. This is not just a conclusion, but a celebration of the wisdom and wit shared by the diverse guests who have graced *The Shop*. Their words, rich with experience and honesty, have illuminated the show and left an indelible mark on our understanding of the intricate tapestry of sports, culture, and life.

These quotes represent more than just fleeting moments of dialogue; they are the essence of personal truths and universal realities. They've sparked conversations, inspired actions, and influenced how we perceive and interact with the world around us in many ways. As we revisit these memorable phrases, we're reminded of the show's unique ability to strip away the celebrity facade and reveal the genuine human experiences.

In *The Shop*, candidness is not just a format but a philosophy. The show has consistently provided a space where vulnerability meets strength, where personal battles become communal discussions, and where laughter intertwines with profound realizations. The quotes that have emerged are testaments to the show's unfiltered nature, offering raw, unadorned glimpses into the minds and hearts of its guests.

In closing this book, we celebrate *The Shop* not just as a show but as a cultural phenomenon that has redefined the art of conversation. Its legacy is etched in the impactful discussions that took place and the lasting impressions these discussions have left on us as viewers and readers. As you immerse yourself in the echoes of wisdom from *The Shop*, may you find inspiration, resonance, and a renewed appreciation for the power of open, honest dialogue.

SEASON 6, EPISODE 4, LOS ANGELES, CA

AMIRA
TVLogic
DIONIC
XT

"You know, when I graduated from college, the average salary for a journalist was $19,000 a year. So, we came in with the expectation we were supposed to be broke and in this for a noble reason. When I first became a sports columnist, I was at the *Orlando Sentinel*. And I was the only Black female sports columnist at a daily newspaper in North America. But when I became a better businesswoman, I became a better journalist. So, I tell young journalists coming up, don't be afraid to make a business decision at all because a profession may manipulate you."

JEMELE HILL
SEASON 4, EPISODE 3, MIAMI, FL

F*ck It,
I'M

"Healing is not permanent because you can still get triggered. I can feel something. I'll know if I'm triggered by something. I'll be like, 'Wait a minute, Tab, you about to react in a way that you shouldn't react.' Right? And so, I just take a moment. Anytime we react out of emotion is most times not the right reaction. You just ain't processed it yet."

TABITHA BROWN
SEASON 6, EPISODE 4,
NEW YORK CITY, NY

"Choices are not binary.

Life is not a multiple choice.

You make it what it is."

NNEKA OGWUMIKE
SEASON 4, EPISODE 1,
LOS ANGELES, CA

"All the roles that I've played; I love them. Though they might have a hard exterior, they're really warm and loving inside. And so, people could say 'Oh I like her. I like that.' And there's this idea that female characters have to be likable [in film and TV]. And I was like, man, I don't want to put myself in that box."

DOMINQUE FISHBACK
SEASON 6, EPISODE 7, LOS ANGELES, CA

“I was just like, that’s never happening again. I may lose again. I may not win everything. But I will never, I will never fail at anything.”

LEBRON JAMES
SEASON 4, EPISODE 1, LOS ANGELES, CA

"If you're really good,
your greatest failure
is the beginning
of the greatest thing
in your life."

MAVERICK CARTER
SEASON 4, EPISODE 1, LOS ANGELES, CA

THE × SHOP

SEASON 7, EPISODE 2, LAS VEGAS, NV

"You should own your publishing and it should be an admin deal.

You should own your masters and it should be a licensing deal. Like, the ownership part should be done. If that's not done, then we have a lot more work to do as a society.

I just believe today that creators, the momentum is behind you.

. . . So, creators, how do you now put yourself in position because now you're replacing cable channels?

What are you doing to be prepared for that opportunity?"

STEVE STOUTE
SEASON 6, EPISODE 2, SALT LAKE CITY, UT

“I’d rather fail being who I am than fail being somebody that they want me to be.”

LEBRON JAMES
SEASON 2, EPISODE 4, LOS ANGELES, CA

A'JA WILSON
AMBER
JADAKISS
Hello my name is
CARMELO ANTHONY
TRAE
5
CHASE
4
Hello my name is
PAUL RIVERA
MAVERICK
LEBRON
IDRIS
STEVE STOUTE
DRAYMOND
FAT JOE

ABOUT THE AUTHOR

ERNEST WILKINS is a seasoned writer with expertise spanning cultural critique, advertising, and personal essays. With over a decade of experience, he's shaped culturally resonant narratives for global giants like Nike, Twitter, Twitch, Red Bull, and Jordan Brand. His pen has graced the pages of top publications, including *GQ*, *Rolling Stone*, *Pitchfork*, *New York Magazine*, and the *Chicago Tribune*.

Beyond his commercial work, Ernest is the mastermind behind *Office Hours Mag*, a newsletter for the culturally curious, and *Gameday Grails*, a treasure trove for vintage sportswear enthusiasts. When the day's work ends, Ernest cherishes time with his family and crafting intricate playlists.

Whether it's copywriting, crafting editorial strategies, or diving deep into audio, Ernest's multifaceted talents shine through, making him a force to reckon with in the world of storytelling.

A FEW FUN TIDBITS: Indie rock icon Andrew WK taught him how to ride a bike, and he's left his mark on pop culture with contributions to memes and appearances on shows like ABC's *Supermarket Sweep*.

GUCCI
LAKERS

B CAM - ROCHELLE
F CAM - NINA
UMD 11
L CAM- REBECA

D CAM - HOOD
H CAM - KOMODO
UMD 12

INSIGHT EDITIONS

PO Box 3088
San Rafael, CA 94912
www.insighteditions.com

Find us on Facebook: www.facebook.com/InsightEditions
Follow us on Instagram: @insighteditions

PAGE 19 - Teenie Harris Archive/Carnegie Museum of Art / Contributor
PAGE 108 - Bettmann / Contributor

Library of Congress Cataloging-in-Publication Data available.

ISBN: 979-8-88663-426-6

Publisher: Raoul Goff
VP, Co-Publisher: Vanessa Lopez
VP, Creative Director: Chrissy Kwasnik
Publishing Director: Mike Degler
Executive Editor: Jennifer Sims
Editorial Assistant: Jeff Chiarelli
Senior Project Editor: Nora Milman
VP, Manufacturing: Alix Nicholaeff
Senior Production Manager: Greg Steffen
Senior Production Manager, Subsidiary Rights: Lina s Palma-Tenema

ROOTS of PEACE REPLANTED PAPER
Insight Editions, in association with Roots of Peace, will plant two trees for each tree used in the manufacturing of this book. Roots of Peace is an internationally renowned humanitarian organization dedicated to eradicating land mines worldwide and converting war-torn lands into productive farms and wildlife habitats. Roots of Peace will plant two million fruit and nut trees in Afghanistan and provide farmers there with the skills and support necessary for sustainable land use.

Manufactured in China by Insight Editions

10 9 8 7 6 5 4 3 2 1

PHOTOGRAPHERS

The Shop Pilot Episodes 1-3, Raven Varona • The Shop Season 1, Episode 1, HBO, Jack Johnson • The Shop Season 1, Episode 2, HBO, Zach Dilgard • The Shop Season 1, Episode 3, HBO, Alexis Cuarexma • The Shop Season 2, Episode 1, Nolis Anderson • The Shop Season 2, Episode 2, Geffen Shichor • The Shop Season 2, Episode 4, Danielle Alston • The Shop Season 2, Episode 5-6, Quinn Murphy • The Shop Season 3, Episode 1, Nolis Anderson • The Shop Season 3, Episode 2, Danielle Alston • The Shop Season 4, Episode 1, Danielle Alston • The Shop Season 4, Episode 2, 6, Bexx Francois • The Shop Season 4, Episode 3, Nolis Anderson • The Shop Season 4, Episode 4-5, Quinn Murphy • The Shop Season 5, Episode 1, 8, Danielle Alston • The Shop Season 5, Episode 2, Akilah T. • The Shop Season 5, Episode 3, 7, Bexx Francois • The Shop Season 5, Episode 4-6, Quinn Murphy • The Shop Season 6, Episodes 1-8, Bexx Francois • The Shop Season 7, Episode 2, Quinn Murphy • The Shop Season 7, Episode 4, Bexx Francois

THE SPRINGHILL COMPANY

LeBron James, *Chairman, The SpringHill Company, Executive Producer, The Shop*
Maverick Carter, *CEO, The SpringHill Company*
Paul Rivera, *Co-Creator and GM, The Shop*
Randy Mims, *Co-Creator, The Shop*
Caroline Randaccio, *Sr. Director, The Shop*
Lauren Chandler, *Brand Manager, The Shop*
Daniel Krueger, *Creative Director, The Shop*
Cody Moore, *Design Lead, The Shop*
Marcus Blackwell, *Sr. Writer, The Shop*
Lauren Bruno, *Art Director, The Shop*
Ricardo Viramontes, *Chief Creative Officer, The Springhill Company*
Albert Park, *Senior Vice President, Business & Legal Affairs*
Ed Telarroja, *Director, Franchise Talent*
Alexa Meltzer, *Chief of Staff of the CEO*
Jimmy Spencer, *SVP, Talent Partnerships*
Jessica Shelley, *Director, Production - Franchise*
Katie Kimes, *Production Coordinator*

SPECIAL THANKS

Rich Paul
Lionel "Brownie Blendz" Harris
Nick "Slick" Castellanos
Vince "The Barber" Garcia
Frēhand
JT Simon